TREES ROCK!

People – Environment – Animals

Roger F. Hartwich Jr.   M.S.E., M.S.

Trees Rock: People – Environment – Animals

First Print Edition

Copyright @ 2021 RFH-RLP Real Life Publishing, LLC

All rights reserved. No part of this book may be reproduced or transmitted in any form by any means, electronic or mechanical, including photocopying, recording, or by any information storage and retrieval system without the written permission of the author, except when permitted by law.

Disclaimer: This publication contains material primarily for educational and informational purposes. The author and publisher have made earnest effort to ensure that the information in this book was correct at publication time and do not assume and hereby disclaim any liability to any party for any loss, damage, disruption caused by errors and omissions.

Cover and Interior Design by Simon Goodway

ISBN: 978-1-7362828-1-6

Table of Contents

Preface

1. Kinds of Trees
2. Clean Air
3. Slow Climate Change and Global Warming
4. Clean Water
5. Erosion Control
6. Home for Birds
7. Wildlife Habitat: Food, Shelter, and Home for Animals
8. Fruit
9. Nuts
10. Maple Syrup
11. Save Energy: Shade to Cool Our Homes
12. Screen from Roads, Highways, and Neighbors
13. Beauty in the Landscape, Forest, and Yard
14. Places to Walk, Hike, Picnic, and Play
15. Wood Products: Good for the Economy
16. Paper and Paper Products: Good for the Economy
17. Jobs and Careers for People: Good for the Economy and Source of Income
18. Tree: A Living Memorial

Summary/Conclusion

Worksheet: Discussion Questions

Worksheet: Fill in the Blank

About the Author

Preface

The purpose of this book is to teach youth, in simple terms, why trees "rock," in other words, about all the good things trees do for us and why we need trees. This book emphasizes the importance and value of trees to people and society, the economy, the environment including clean air and clean water, and birds and animals. It is hoped that this book will educate and inspire youth to think about trees and all the benefits they provide to our quality of life, and why we need to plant, preserve, and care for trees. It is also hoped that this book will motivate youth to become present and future tree planters, nurturers, and investors in trees for their generation as adults, and future generations that follow.

1   Kinds of Trees

There are many kinds of trees. **Deciduous** (de-sij-'oo) trees lose their leaves annually, usually in the late fall. These trees include maple, oak, birch, elm, fruit, nut, flowering crab trees, and very many others. **Evergreen** cone-bearing trees keep their needles year-round. They include pines, spruce, fir, and cedar trees.

2   Clean Air

Trees help to clean the air by filtering dirt and dust particles from factories and power plants, and auto emissions from cars and trucks. Air pollution can also come from volcanoes and wildfires. Trees can absorb or take in air pollutants through their leaves. Removing pollution improves air quality and human health.

Trees also absorb or take in carbon dioxide gas from our atmosphere and give off oxygen for people to breathe.

3   Slow Climate Change and Global Warming

Trees help to slow climate change. **Global warming** is the rising of the earth's surface temperature, due mainly to the increase of Carbon Dioxide and other greenhouse gases in the atmosphere. Greenhouse gases in the atmosphere are mainly caused by burning fossil fuels including oil, natural gas, and coal.

Climate change is the warming and many side effects of the warming, including melting glaciers, heavier rainstorms, and more frequent drought. More powerful, intense storms may occur. Also, with global warming, sea levels rise which can cause destructive flooding.

Climate change includes increasing changes in the measures of climate over a long period of time, including rainfall, temperature, wind patterns, and length of seasons.

4   Clean water

Trees help to keep water clean for drinking, and our lakes and rivers clean for swimming and boating. Lake, river, stream, and ocean water can also be kept cleaner for fish to live in.

Trees in our yards, parks, and forests absorb water through their roots and slow the flow of water into the soil. This helps to reduce water from going into lakes, rivers, and streams, and may help to reduce floods into homes and land.

5   Erosion Control

Tree roots help hold the soil in place when it rains and prevent **erosion**, the washing away of the soil.

6   Home and Food for Birds

Trees provide places for birds to build nests and live safely. Some trees also provide food including fruit, nuts, and berries for birds to eat.

7 Habitat: Food, Shelter, and Home for Animals

Trees provide homes and food for animals, including deer, bear, wolves, foxes, small animals such as rabbits and squirrels, and birds such as eagles and grouse. Food would include pine needles, leaves, nuts, and berries.

8   Fruit for People to Eat

Fruit trees provide people with many kinds of nutritious and healthy fruit to eat, including apples, pears, peaches, lemons, plums, cherries, and bananas. The sale of fruit at orchards, grocery stores, and at farmers' markets is also good for the economy.

9   Nuts for People to Eat

Nut trees provide people with nutritious, healthy nuts to eat. These include walnuts, almonds, cashews, pecans, pistachios, hazelnuts, and others. The sale of nuts in grocery stores is also good for the economy.

10   Maple Syrup

Maple trees provide us with delicious maple syrup. Maple trees are tapped in early spring. We use maple syrup on pancakes, waffles, and French toast.

11   Save Energy: Shade to Cool Our Homes

Trees provide shade to help cool our homes from the sun during hot summer days. Trees help to save energy and lower energy costs. This is good for our economy and saves people money.

12   Screen from Roads, Highways, and Neighbors

Trees provide privacy screens for homes from busy roads, highways, and neighbors. Trees also help to reduce noise from noisy cars and trucks.

13 Beauty in the Landscape, Forest, and Yard

Flowering crab trees provide beautiful pink, red, and white colored flowers in spring. Some Maple trees provide bright colored leaves of red and orange in fall, while other Maples provide dark purple leaves in summer. Other trees provide bright yellow leaves in fall. Evergreen trees including spruce, pine, fir, and cedar provide beautiful green or blue-green color in the landscape. Trees are beautiful in yards, neighborhoods, parks, along roads, and in the forest.

14 Places to Walk, Hike, Picnic, and Play

Trees provide beautiful places in our yards and parks, near lakes, streams, rivers, and mountains, to picnic, walk, jog, hike, and play. Trees are good for our health and well-being.

15   Wood Products: Good for the Economy

Trees provide wood to build homes, barns, and other buildings, furniture, cabinets, baseball bats, pencils, and many other things made of wood. With these uses of trees, trees are good for our economy.

16   Paper and Paper Products: Good for the Economy

Paper also comes from trees. To make paper, raw wood is turned into pulp, which is made from wood fibers and chemicals that are mixed together. Machines grind wood chips into pulp, or chemicals are used to make pulp. Liquid in the pulp is then removed to make paper. Wet paper is squeezed to get the water out. Then heat is used to further dry the paper.

It takes many years for trees to grow. It is very important to conserve paper by recycling paper and paper products. Many products that we use today are made from recycled paper.

The production and sale of paper and paper products are good for our economy.

17 Jobs and Careers: Good for the Economy and Source of Income

Trees provide many jobs, occupations, and careers for people to earn a living. These include garden center owners and workers, carpenters, foresters, loggers, lumber yard workers, paper mill workers, arborists, tree nursery growers, landscapers, landscape designers, landscape architects, Christmas tree growers, fruit and nut tree growers, grocery and furniture store owners, and sales people. Trees are good for our economy.

18   Tree: A Living Memorial

A tree, or more than one tree, can be planted as a living memorial to a family member, relative, friend, or loved one in their memory. The tree will be a living tribute to remember and honor the person who has passed away.

Summary/Conclusion

What would the world be like without trees? How would people, animals, and the environment be affected and different without trees? If we had no or far fewer trees on earth, what would the air and water be like? Would we be able to breathe as well? Would there be more air and water pollution? More floods? What would life be like with less or no fruit and nuts from trees to eat? What if we had much less wood from trees to build houses and furniture, or less paper to use in our homes, offices, businesses, and schools?

Trees "rock" because they are very valuable and provide benefits to our lives in many ways. Trees affect our environment, our health, happiness, and quality of life. Trees help to provide clean air, clean water, and slow the rate of climate change. Trees provide food and homes for birds and animals.

Trees provide people with fruit and nuts to eat, privacy screening, wood to build our homes, and places to picnic, hike, and play. Deciduous trees provide beauty in the landscape, many with beautiful flowers in the spring and brightly colored leaves in the fall. Evergreen trees provide beautiful dark green or bluish green needles, shelter for animals, and protection for our homes from cold winter winds.

Trees also "rock" because they shade our homes from the sun during hot summer days, help to cool our homes, and save energy. Trees provide many people with jobs and careers from which they earn income and make a living. Trees are good for our economy. We need trees.

What can you do? Become interested in trees and learn about many of the good things that trees provide. Learn about the Amazon Rainforest, why trees are disappearing and being cut down by the thousands, and how that may affect people, plants, animals, and our climate. Learn about what is happening to trees in your own country and in other countries, and about tree planting and reforestation efforts. Learn how to plant and care for trees. As you grow older, you may wish to join and help organizations that grow trees and support tree planting in communities, cities, parks and forests in our country and around the world.

Worksheet: Discussion Questions

1. Name several kinds of trees you know about or like? Describe some interesting things about them.

2. What are trees called that lose their leaves every year? What trees keep their needles all year long?

3. How do trees help to keep our air clean and easier to breathe, air that is better for our health?

4. How do trees help to prevent erosion?

5. How do trees help to keep water clean?

6. Why are trees good for birds and animals? How do trees benefit birds and animals?

7. Name some healthy fruit from fruit trees.

8. Name some healthy nuts from nut trees.

9. How do we get maple syrup from maple trees? When are maple trees tapped for maple syrup?

10. How do trees help us save energy in our homes?

11. What are some other ways trees help us in our landscapes, yards, around our homes, and along roads and highways?

12. Name some of the many things made of wood that we get from trees.

13. Where does paper come from? How is paper made? Name several paper products made from wood.

14. List some jobs, occupations, and careers related to trees from which people can earn a living. Why are trees good for our economy?

Worksheet: Fill in the Blank

Word Bank

Maple   Evergreens   Walnuts   Almonds   Erosion   Apples   Oranges   Pears   Plums   Bananas   Air   Water   Deciduous   Climate Change   Forester   Carpenter   Landscaper   Arborist   Tree Nursery Grower

1. Trees help provide clean _____ and clean _____.

2. Trees that lose their leaves each year: _____.

3. Trees that keep their needles all year long: _____.

4. _____ trees give us Maple syrup.

5. Five different kinds of fruit from fruit trees:

   _____, _____, _____, _____, _____.

6. Two kinds of nuts from nut trees:

   _____, _____.

7. Five occupations or careers that involve people working with trees: _____,

   _____, _____, _____,

   _____.

8. Trees can help the environment by slowing the rate of _____.

9. Tree roots can hold the soil in place and prevent the washing away of the soil, called

   _____.

About the Author

Roger F. Hartwich Jr., M.S.E., M.S. B.S., B.A., has been a teacher and a landscaper/landscape designer/horticulturist/arborist for many years. Roger has taught full time K-12 Special Education and regular elementary education, and most subject areas, including German, as a K-12 substitute teacher. Roger has owned/ operated a horticultural services/landscaping company for many years, and has worked as a horticulturist/head groundskeeper for a large institution. He has also worked in financial services for a short period of time. Roger has strong interest in environmental preservation, trees and many other plants, horticulture, arboriculture, and landscape design as well as financial literacy.

Roger is an Army veteran and former Navy Reservist, Navy Reserve Retired, with 20 years of military service. Roger holds Masters' Degrees in Special Education and Recreation and Park Administration, a B.S. Degree in Elementary Education, a B.A. Degree in Social Science, German minor, and a technical college degree in horticulture/landscape technology and design.

Roger believes in relating and applying learning to real life skills. He has written this book for youth about trees, their critical value and importance to people and society, the economy, environment, and birds and animals. It is hoped that this book will educate, inspire, and motivate youth to become interested in trees, future tree planters, nurturers, and supporters of organizations involved with tree growing, reforestation, and planting in neighborhoods, towns, cities, parks and forests throughout the world.

www.ingramcontent.com/pod-product-compliance
Lightning Source LLC
Chambersburg PA
CBHW042255100526
44589CB00002B/32